# Be Smart About Your Future

## RISK MANAGEMENT AND INSURANCE

**RISK AHEAD**

BE SMART
ABOUT
MONEY
AND
FINANCIAL
LITERACY

**Enslow Publishers, Inc.**
40 Industrial Road
Box 398
Berkeley Heights, NJ 07922
USA

http://www.enslow.com

Nothing herein is intended or shall be construed as legal advice or as a recommendation for or against any particular product or business. All names in hypothetical problems are fictitious and are not intended as a representation of any particular person or business.

**Library of Congress Cataloging-in-Publication Data**

Graham, Amy.
  Be smart about your future : risk management and insurance / Amy Graham.
    pages cm — (Be smart about money and financial literacy)
  Includes index.
  Summary: "Discusses risk management and insurance, including identifying risk, understanding the different types of insurance, examining the parts of an auto insurance policy, and making smart decisions to protect your financial life in the future"—Provided by publisher.
  Audience: Age 14–18.
  Audience: Grade 9–12.
  ISBN 978-0-7660-4285-8
  1. Insurance—United States—Juvenile literature. 2. Risk (Insurance)—United States—Juvenile literature. 3. Risk management—United States—Juvenile literature. I. Title.
  HG8531.G697 2014
  368.00973—dc23
                          2013011669
Future editions:
Paperback ISBN: 978-1-4644-0519-8
EPUB ISBN: 978-1-4645-1265-0
Single-User PDF ISBN: 978-1-4646-1265-7
Multi-User PDF ISBN: 978-0-7660-5897-2

Printed in the United States of America
112013 Bang Printing, Brainerd, Minn.
10 9 8 7 6 5 4 3 2 1

**To Our Readers:** We have done our best to make sure all Internet addresses in this book were active and appropriate when we went to press. However, the author and the publisher have no control over and assume no liability for the material available on those Internet sites or on other Web sites they may link to. Any comments or suggestions can be sent by e-mail to comments@enslow.com or to the address on the back cover.

♻ Enslow Publishers, Inc., is committed to printing our books on recycled paper. The paper in every book contains 10% to 30% post-consumer waste (PCW). The cover board on the outside of each book contains 100% PCW. Our goal is to do our part to help young people and the environment too!

**Clipart Credits:** Shutterstock.com

**Cover Illustration:** Shutterstock.com (Ulysses S. Grant) and Comstock / Photos.com (black suit).

# Contents

Throughout the book, look for this logo 😊 for smart financial tips and this logo 😵 for bad choices to avoid. Also, don't forget to "Do the Math" at the end of each chapter.

# Hard Times

James always thought he led the typical life of an American teenager. He got average grades, played on his high school soccer team, and enjoyed hanging out with his friends on the weekends. His family did not have a lot of money, but his parents were hard workers. There always seemed to be enough to cover the family's needs.

Then when James was sixteen, something happened that changed his life forever. His father, Paul, had a heart attack after returning from one of his daily morning runs. By the time the ambulance arrived, the EMTs were unable to resuscitate him. Paul was pronounced dead upon arrival at the hospital.

Over the following weeks and months, James and his sisters grieved the loss of their father. Their mother was completely overcome with sorrow and shock at the death of her husband. Neither she nor Paul had seriously considered the possibility that he would die in his thirties. As a result, they had not made financial plans for the family in case of his death.

The family had some money set aside in savings and that covered the costs of the funeral service. James's mother had a part-time job, but she did not make enough money to cover the family's expenses. She knew she had to find a full-time job; however, she was so overwhelmed with grief that she found it difficult to go about her day much less begin a job search.

As the oldest child, James felt responsible for his family. He found a job in a warehouse and worked after school and on weekends. He turned his checks over to his mom to help pay the bills. Even with this extra income, the family could no longer afford to make the mortgage payments to the bank. None of them wanted to leave their home where they had many happy family memories.

As they struggled to make enough to pay for their groceries, it soon became clear that they had no choice but to move. They sold their home, packed their belongings, and moved to a small apartment they could afford. James's younger sisters were sad to move away from their friends and neighbors. James looks back at that time in his life as the hardest thing he and his family have ever been through.

After a year, James's mother found full-time work and things began looking up. James graduated from high school and attended a nearby community college to get a business degree. He continued to take part-time jobs in college to help support his family. James, his sisters, and his mom remain a close-knit family. James has decided to become a non-fee financial planner. He wants to help others to avoid the experience he and his family went through after his father's death.

## Managing Risk

Occasionally, life reminds us of how unpredictable it can be. Sudden loss, when it strikes, is devastating. One day, life is going along in a routine way and the next—BAM! Everything is turned on its head. What are you supposed to do? Cower in a corner? Live in denial that anything bad could ever happen to you? Neither approach will do you much good. So what can you do?

You can learn about making wise financial decisions. You can learn to limit the risks you take and protect your assets. Your assets are the things you have that are valuable to you. Assets can be things you own: money in the bank, your home, or your car. Assets can also be things that are priceless to you though they may have no economic value: your health and your family.

You can figure out your tolerance for risk. How much risk are you comfortable with? Let's face it. No one would reach his goals if he did not take risks. On the other hand, people who engage in risky behaviors without considering the consequences are flirting with disaster. The decisions you make in life will determine how much risk you face. People have different comfort levels with risk, or risk tolerance. You will find the balance that works best for you.

**Visit** the Life Foundation's Web site at www.lifehappens.org. Its mission? To help people understand the importance of insurance. There, you can read real-life stories of how smart planning saved people from situations they never dreamed they would face.

**"It** will never happen to me." No one wants to think that the worst could happen to him. But the truth is, no one knows what the future will bring. So don't plan your life around the idea that it will never happen to you. Make sure you have a contingency plan, just in case.

**Be Smart About Your Future**

Now it's your turn to "Do the Math." The end of each chapter features a math or word problem. Use what you learned in the chapter to help you answer the questions. The right math will help you make the right financial decisions.

# Do the Math

Choose an item from the list below and explain why you think it would be important to purchase insurance for it. Pick a different item from the list that you think does not need insurance. Explain why you think so.

- New laptop for college
- Motorcycle
- Canoe
- Diamond engagement ring
- Your luggage during a two-week vacation to Italy
- Bicycle
- New flat-screen television with surround sound system

# Insurance to the Rescue

Misfortunes happen somewhere, to someone, every single day. You fall on the ski slope, breaking your leg. A car rear-ends your car at a traffic light, crushing your back bumper. No matter how cautious you are, setbacks—small or large—will happen to you. Welcome to the world: There is a certain amount of risk in life. But wouldn't it be great if there were a way to protect yourself from the financial loss these setbacks bring? What if there was a way to pay your unexpected doctor bills? Replace your car's smashed bumper? What if you could handle all these setbacks without suddenly having to come up with extra money? Good news. There is. It is called insurance.

## Insurance: A Tool in Your Financial Toolbox

Insurance is a tool that people use to help manage their finances. An insurance policy protects you in case you suffer a loss. So what kind of loss are we talking about? Well, that depends. There are different kinds of insurance. Health insurance can cover you when you need to see a doctor or buy a prescription from the pharmacy. Homeowners insurance covers you when your house is damaged. Life insurance covers a family when the income provider dies. Travel insurance covers you when you travel and your wallet or luggage is stolen. If you can lose it, there is probably some company out there willing to insure it.

Of course, it wouldn't make sense to insure everything you own. (Hello? Yes, I'd like to take out an insurance policy on my socks. That's right: I'm only ever able to find one and not the other. How much would that cost? Really? Okay, never mind.) Ask yourself: Would I suffer financially if I lost this, or could I replace it? Is it something I could live without? If it would cause a serious financial hardship to lose it, then you should insure it.

As a teen, you probably don't yet have many assets that need to be insured. However, you have most likely had experience with one kind of insurance: health insurance. You may not have given it much thought because you are probably on your parents' or guardians' policy. When you visit the doctor, chances are they ask to see your health insurance card. There is another kind of insurance that is applicable to teens. If you drive, or plan to get a driver's license in the near future, you need to know about auto insurance.

# How an Insurance Policy Works

An insurance policy is a legal contract between you and your insurance company. You agree to pay money called a premium to your insurance company. In return, your insurance company agrees to cover you in the case of a loss. Premiums are typically paid monthly, biannually (twice a year), or annually. In the event that you suffer a loss, for example, a car accident in which your car is destroyed, you contact your insurance agency to report a claim. A claim is a request for payment under the terms of your policy. Your insurance agency reviews your claim and pays you what you are due. In this example, if they agree your car cannot be salvaged, they would pay to replace your car.

Insurance policies, like all contracts, have fine print to read and understand before you sign. Not all insurance policies are created equal. Insurance companies are businesses. Like all businesses, they are in the market to make a profit. Some are more reputable than others. To get the most for your money, you'll want to have a clear understanding of what you need in an insurance policy. Then you should shop around.

You've probably seen ads for many of America's major insurance companies: Geico, Progressive, State Farm, Liberty Mutual, Nationwide, and Allstate to name a few. There are reputable smaller companies that don't advertise nationally. Some companies specialize in helping certain groups of people. For example, AARP offers insurance to people over the age of fifty. Horace Mann and TIAA-CREF are examples of companies that offer insurance to people who work in the field of education.

As with any important purchase you make, you should do your research. Explain to the insurance agent what you need. The agent will give you a quote—that is, an estimate of how much your premium would cost for a policy. Take your time, compare quotes, and make an informed decision. And remember: Your insurance company is who you'll be dealing with if you get in an accident. If that happens, you will be under a lot of stress. Make sure you are doing business with people you trust to help you in an emergency.

# Something for ... Nothing?

You may be asking yourself, "Wait a minute. So I pay a premium to my insurance company for insurance. Let's say I am careful and with a bit of luck I never get in an accident. Do I get my money back?" The answer there is "No." Is that fair? Yes, in fact, it is if you think about it. Your money purchased peace of mind. You did not have to worry about what would happen if you got in an accident. You were covered. Having insurance is good for the community at large, too. The roads are a safer place when every driver is insured.

# Pay Now or Pay Later: Choosing a Deductible

Every insurance policy has a deductible. This is the amount of the loss that you agree to pay out of your own pocket. Once you have paid the deductible, the insurance company covers the remainder of the loss. For example, you are in a car accident, and there is

$40,000 worth of damage. Your insurance policy states you have a $500 deductible per claim. You must first pay $500 toward the cost of repairing your car. Then your insurance company pays the remaining balance of $39,500.

If you want to save money on your premium, look into increasing your deductible. The higher your deductible, the less expensive your insurance premium will be. That's because you are agreeing to pay for smaller claims and your insurance company is only footing the bill for larger expenses. But be careful! Don't choose a deductible that you won't be able to afford. The whole point of insurance is to be there when you need it most.

**Be Smart About Your Future**

**It** can be daunting to get your yearly insurance bill for hundreds of dollars. Instead of scrambling to come up with the money each year, divide your annual premium by twelve. This will tell you how much your insurance costs per month. Then set aside that amount each month in a bank account. When your bill comes, you won't have to think twice about how you will pay for it.

**You** want to pay the least amount of money possible for your auto insurance. You find a policy that costs you very little. Then you get into an accident and realize you have to pay a $5,000 deductible before your insurance kicks in. So much for saving money! Instead, choose a deductible that you will be able to afford. You may have to pay a bit more for your premium, but you will save a lot in the event that you get into an accident—and that's the whole point of insurance.

**Insurance to the Rescue**

# Do the Math

C Which auto insurance policy would better meet the needs of a student with a part-time job? Why?

C Policy A costs $300 per year with a $1,000 deductible per incident.

Policy B costs $550 per year with a $250 annual deductible.

C

Be Smart About Your Future

# Auto Insurance

It's the law—you need auto insurance in most states. Even in the states that do not require it, drivers must pay a fee or put up a cash bond if they choose not to purchase auto insurance (except in New Hampshire). When you get behind the wheel of a car, you need to have a way to pay for damages if you should cause an accident. Likewise, you want to know that the other drivers on the road will be able to pay you should they cause an accident. According to the U.S. Census Bureau, there were 10.8 million motor vehicle accidents in the United States in 2009 alone.

When police officers pull over a driver, they ask for proof of insurance, a driver's license, and car registration. Anyone caught driving without auto insurance has to pay a fine. Do it more than once and you face tougher consequences. You could lose your license and have your car's registration revoked. The state could even impound your car. With that kind of driving record, good luck trying to buy auto insurance in the future. Your insurance company will consider you a high-risk driver—one that is likely to cost them too much money. Once your policy runs out, they may not allow you to renew it. If you are able to find a company willing to issue you a special "high-risk driver" policy, the cost will be through the roof.

Yet some drivers, in a desperate attempt to cut costs during hard economic times, take the gamble and drive uninsured. The Insurance Research Council estimates that one in seven drivers on the road did not have insurance in 2011.

## Liability Insurance

Whose fault was it? That is often the question when an accident occurs. If the accident is determined to be your fault, then you are liable for the costs. Most states require drivers to have basic liability insurance. That way, if you are responsible for an accident, you will be able to pay for any damages. Your insurance company will pay for any damages you cause to others. What if you don't have liability insurance? Then you are responsible.

## Uninsured/Underinsured Drivers

What happens when you get in an accident, and the other driver is not insured? If you only have liability insurance, you will have to pay for any damage to your car. You will also have to pay for your medical bills if you are hurt. You may have the option to sue the other driver to reclaim some of the money you've lost, but—and this should come as no surprise—people who don't bother to buy auto insurance rarely have any money anyway. You are unlikely to reclaim your losses by suing.

Some states require you to purchase uninsured/underinsured motorist coverage. That way, if you are in an accident with an uninsured motorist, you will have help from your insurance company. It may not seem fair to have to pay for your own insurance as well as for an uninsured driver. In truth, it isn't fair. But insurance isn't about fairness. It is about protecting yourself and getting back on your feet with as little cost as possible after an accident.

# Collision and Comprehensive Insurance

If you get into an accident, liability insurance will pay for the costs of damage you may cause to other people's property. What about the damage to your car? Liability insurance does not pay for that. That is why you will want additional insurance coverage, especially if you are still paying a loan for your car. There's nothing worse than owing the bank for a totaled car.

To cover the costs of repairing or replacing your car, you need to buy collision insurance. What if your car is stolen or damaged in a natural disaster? You need comprehensive insurance to cover those scenarios. Personal Injury Protection coverage pays if you or anyone in your car is injured in an accident. You'll need to think carefully about what kind of insurance package makes the most sense for you. You can purchase a policy for various amounts of liability, collision, comprehensive, uninsured motorist, and personal injury protection. The more coverage you choose, the higher your premium will be. If you choose less coverage, your policy premium will be cheaper. Your insurance agent can help you find the right balance.

## Proof of Insurance

Once you pay your premium, your insurance company sends you proof of insurance. This may be in the form of an insurance card or a simple paper certificate. You will want to keep this handy in your car. You'll need proof of insurance when you go to register your car. You will also need it on hand if you are pulled over by police or if you are in an accident. It should tell you what to do if you are involved in an accident, including how to report the accident and what information you will need.

## Multi–Driver Policy

If you get your driver's license while you live with your parents, your best deal might be to get added to their auto insurance policy. However, if your parents drive new or expensive cars, this may end up costing them more than putting you on your own policy for a modest car. If you will only be driving one of the family's vehicles, your parents can limit your insurance coverage to that vehicle. That can save a considerable amount of money. Only choose this option if you won't be driving any of the family's other cars.

**Be Smart About Your Future**

# Dude, Where's My Car?

If your car is broken into or stolen, talk to the police. Then call your insurance company to report the theft. They will wait a set number of days to see if the police are able to locate your car. If your car does not turn up, they will cut you a check for the market value of the car. If the police find your car badly damaged, your policy will pay for the damage (minus any deductible). It may be too damaged to fix. In that case, they will declare it totaled and send you a check for the market value of your car. If the damage is not too bad, you might be better off to pay for the damage yourself rather than file a claim with your insurance company. You will want to consider how much your deductible is. But remember, if you do not have comprehensive insurance, your policy will not cover theft.

**If** you're hoping to drive your parents' car, talk to them about getting on their insurance policy. Call the insurance agent to find out how much it will cost to add you. Then come up with a plan for how you can pay for it through your allowance or part-time job. Your parents will be impressed with your level of maturity. This will help them to see you are ready for the responsibilities that come with driving a car.

**Drive** your parent's car even though you don't have insurance. What are the chances you'll get pulled over? Bad idea. You need to be covered by an insurance policy before you get behind the wheel of a car. Otherwise, you could get caught and face a fine plus higher insurance costs.

**Be Smart About Your Future**

# Do the Math

You are a full-time student with a part-time job. You were able to pay for your first car in full with money you saved. You did not have to take out a loan, which was important as you don't make a lot of money. The car's not worth much, but it is all yours. Now it is time to insure it. Compare the two auto insurance policies below. List three major differences between the two policies. Choose the best one for your car and explain why you chose it.

## Policy #1

| Description | Limit of liability | Deductible | Premium |
|---|---|---|---|
| Bodily Injury Liability | Each Person $100,000 | | $75.00 |
| | Each Occurrence $300,000 | | |
| Property Damage Liability | Each Occurrence $100,000 | | $60.00 |
| Medical Payments | Each Person $5,000 | | $15.00 |
| Comprehensive | Actual cash value | $250 | $35.00 |
| Collision | Actual cash value | $500 | $110.00 |
| Uninsured Motor Vehicle | Each Person $100,000 | | $15.00 |
| | Each Accident $300,000 | | |
| Total | | $750 | $310 |

## Policy #2

| Description | Limit of liability | Deductible | Premium |
|---|---|---|---|
| Bodily Injury Liability | Each Person $100,000 | | $75.00 |
| | Each Occurrence $300,000 | | |
| Property Damage Liability | Each Occurrence $100,000 | | $60.00 |
| Medical Payments | Each Person $5,000 | | $15.00 |
| Collision | Actual cash value | $1000 | $65.00 |
| Uninsured Motor Vehicle | Each Person $100,000 | | $15.00 |
| | Each Accident $300,000 | | |
| Total | | $1,000 | $230 |

# Lowering Your Auto Insurance Costs

Auto insurance can be expensive for teens and young adults. Your parents may cite this as a reason why you can't drive yet. Read on to find out things you can do to lower your insurance costs. Your parents might be more likely to say yes if you show them you are taking steps to lower the cost.

## Why Does It Cost So Much?

Your age is a big factor. If you are a driver between the ages of sixteen and twenty-six, you pay a higher premium. There is a reason for that: Younger drivers get in more accidents than older drivers. The Center for Disease Control and Prevention reports that the risk of motor vehicle crashes is higher for teens ages 16–19 than any other age group. If you are male, you are going to pay even more. Don't feel randomly discriminated against, guys.

The truth is that men under the age of twenty-five are more than twice as likely as young women to get into an accident. Young men tend to drive faster and are less likely to wear seat belts. They are more likely to engage in reckless behavior, such as driving under the influence of alcohol or drugs.

There's not much you can do to change your age and gender. What you can do is drive carefully and safely. As you gain experience and develop a good driving record, your insurance costs will go down. Many insurance agencies offer a discount once you have driven for several years without an accident or moving violation.

Where you live makes a difference. If you live in a big city with a high theft and collision rate, that will increase the cost of your premium. You may not be able to do much about where you live, but there's a factor you might be able to do something about: the car you drive.

The year, make, and model of your car can make a difference in how much you pay. If your car has a good safety rating, it will be less expensive to insure. New, expensive, and sporty cars cost the most to insure. Luxury cars, such as Mercedes-Benz, Porsche, Jaguar, and BMWs, top the list of the most expensive cars to insure, as they are expensive to repair or replace. The insurance industry also collects statistics on which cars are most often stolen. In 2011, 55,170 Honda Accords (model year 1994) were stolen, making it the number one stolen car in the United States.

If you drive a high-risk car, you will pay more to insure it. When it comes time to buy a car, look for one that is rated high in safety and low in repair costs, and make sure it is not on the list of frequently stolen cars. Call your insurance carrier to get a quote to see how much the car will cost to insure before you buy.

# Ways to Cut Costs on Auto Insurance

- Drive safely. Your insurance rates will drop as you prove you can drive without getting into accidents or getting traffic tickets. Likewise, your rates will rise the more driving errors you make.
- Get good grades. Many insurance agencies offer discounts to good students.
- Take a driving course. Some insurers offer discounts if you take a driver's education course. The more you know, the better driver you will be.
- Don't drive very far? You may qualify for a low-mileage discount. Ask your insurance carrier about other discounts they offer. You may get discounts if your car has extra safety or antitheft features.
- Get several different quotes from insurance companies before you select one. Different companies can offer very different prices. You can save hundreds of dollars by shopping around.

# DUI: Driving Under the Influence

You know never to drink and drive. You might think to yourself "I'm not an idiot. I would never make the decision to drive while drunk." That's easy to say when you are sober, but people make bad decisions when they are drunk. They aren't thinking clearly because alcohol has impaired their brains. In 2011, 9,878 people died in drunk-driving accidents in the United States. Scary, right? That's reason enough not to drink and drive. In addition, once your insurance company hears that you have a DUI, you are flagged as a high-risk driver. Your insurance premium will skyrocket. When it comes time to renew your policy, you may find your insurance company is no longer willing to do business with you.

**Ready** to drive but your parents are dragging their feet when it comes to getting you insured? Show your parents you are ready for the responsibility and willing to help. Contact the insurance company and find out how much it would cost to add you. Then ask how you can lower your insurance premium. Talk with your parents and offer to pay part or all of your share of the insurance costs with your allowance or part-time job earnings.

GOOD ¢

**Who** cares what kind of car you drive, as long as you have a car, right? Think again. The kind of car you drive can make a huge difference in how much your auto insurance costs—not to mention how much it will cost you at the gas pump and paying for repairs and maintenance. Each year, the Insurance Institute for Highway Safety puts out lists of cars and their safety ratings. When it is time to get your first car, look at the car's rating and how much it will cost you . . . before you buy it.

NON ¢

**Be Smart About Your Future**

# Do the Math

Your parents pay $1,500 a year to insure their cars. It will cost an additional $650 per year to add you to their insurance policy. Because you are on the honor roll, you are eligible for a 10% discount. How much will the insurance policy cost per year once they add you?

You decide to take a defensive driving course, knocking another 3% off the total bill. How much will that save?

# Healthy, Wealthy, and Wise

If you've ever had a serious injury or illness, you know how valuable good health is—and how much for granted many of us take it. You could argue that your health is your most precious asset. If you fall sick or are injured, you may not be able to work until you recover. What a terrible combination: no income and mounting doctors' bills. That's why health insurance is one of the most common and important types of insurance.

## How Does Health Insurance Work?

Health insurance may cover the cost of doctor's visits, hospital stays, ambulance rides, medicine from the pharmacy, and many other medical-related items. This is how it works: You pay a premium to your insurance company every month. If you get your health insurance through your work—as many do—your company takes this premium directly out of your paycheck.

When you need to visit the doctor, you may pay nothing or you may owe a co-payment, or co-pay. A co-payment is a small, fixed amount that you must pay each time you visit the doctor or pick up a prescription. The insurance company sets the amount of your co-payment. They also may set an annual deductible. You must pay this amount each year before they begin to cover your bills. If you have an annual deductible, your premium will be less expensive. Once you have reached your deductible, your insurance company pays your doctor's bill.

# Why Does Health Insurance Matter?

Imagine if you were very sick and went to the emergency room, only to be turned away because you didn't have enough money to pay. In some countries, this is how it is. Health care is not a universal right, but a commodity that can be purchased by those with enough money. In other countries, the government provides health care to all citizens. If you have health insurance, you can get the care you need without worrying whether or not you will be able to afford the bill.

# Where Do You Get Health Insurance?

In the United States, most people buy their health insurance through their full-time job. Part-time jobs rarely offer benefits like health insurance. A person can cover his spouse and dependent children on his insurance policies. A dependent child is under age nineteen, or under age twenty-four and a full-time student, or a disabled child of any age. Thanks to the Affordable Health Care Act of 2010, young adults who are not offered health insurance through work can now stay on their parents' insurance policies until the age of twenty-six.

What if your job doesn't offer health-care benefits, and you can't get on your parent's policy? People can buy health insurance through private companies. This can be expensive and is not a viable option for people who don't earn enough. Low-income residents—especially children—may qualify for Medicaid insurance through their state government. Seniors over the age of sixty-five qualify for Medicare. Medicare is the U.S. government's program to provide health insurance for the elderly.

# Insuring Your Good Health and a Long Life

Health insurance is one way to be sure you can afford doctor's visits. However, health insurance doesn't insure good health. The best way to stay healthy is to invest in your health. This kind of investment doesn't cost money. It's about committing to a healthy lifestyle. You can protect your health by respecting your body and treating it right.

# Who Should Buy Life Insurance?

The purpose of life insurance is to continue providing an income in the event that a wage earner dies, leaving his or her dependents without an income. Wondering if you need life insurance? Does anyone depend on you financially? If not, then it is unlikely you need it. Once you have children, a spouse, or elderly parents who depend on the money you earn, you will need an insurance policy.

Life insurance becomes important when you start a family. When you are in your twenties and thirties, death seems far away. Yet this is when a life insurance policy is most necessary. Why? Young families do not yet have much in the way of assets. They are often still paying off loans on their house, cars, even their student loans from college. Home loans, called mortgages, are often thirty-year loans. The death of a wage earner during these years can have devastating financial costs.

As you get older, your need for life insurance should decrease. Eventually, it may disappear altogether. That is because during your lifetime, you will acquire property and save some money. By the time you retire, you can have your loans paid and own your house and your car outright. You will have money in savings. Any children you have will be grown and earning their own incomes. Life insurance may no longer be necessary.

**Buy** life insurance when you are healthy. Life insurance is expensive for people who are old or have preexisting health conditions but very affordable for young, healthy people. You don't need to think about life insurance until you have dependents.

GOOD ¢

NON ¢

**Young** adults who are just starting out on their own sometimes make the decision to go without health insurance. After all, health insurance can cost thousands of dollars a year. What a waste of money when you are young and healthy, right? Wrong. Without health insurance, you won't have access to affordable health care in the event that you fall sick or are in an accident. You need health insurance no matter what your age. Not sure where to look? As a young adult, you should be able to get health insurance through your parents or guardians, your college or school, your job, or Medicaid. Never go without it.

34

# Do the Math

Determine how much money you will owe for a visit to your doctor. The doctor's total bill is $850. You have a $25 co-pay for each visit to the doctor. Your health insurance company pays for 80 percent of your medical bills (not including co-pays) but only after you have met a $1000 annual deductible. So far this year you have paid $500 toward your annual deductible. How much money will you need to pay for this doctor's visit? How much will your insurance company pay?

# Insurance Needs Throughout Your Life

You can insure just about anything if you are willing to pay for it, but here are some more common forms of insurance that can help you to reduce the amount of risk in your life.

## Renters Insurance

When you are a young adult renting your first apartment, you may not give much thought to insuring your stuff. You may not have that much stuff in the first place. But what would happen if you came home one day and your apartment had been broken into by thieves? Your computer, your television, your bike, your stash of emergency cash—all gone. If you have a renters insurance policy, you'd be okay. Most renters policies are not that expensive—for example, $10 a month—depending on how much coverage you choose.

# Homeowners Insurance

When you buy your first home, you will need insurance to cover your house in case something happens to it. In fact, a bank will not loan you the money to buy a house without proof of insurance. The bank takes this wise step to protect its investment.

As with auto insurance, the higher the deductible you choose, the less your homeowners policy premium will cost. If you can afford a deductible of $1,000, you can save as much as 25 percent on your annual premium. Homeowners insurance premiums are typically due once a year.

Common homeowners insurance claims include damage due to water—don't forget to check on the bathtub—and fire, so change the batteries in your smoke detectors regularly. Many policies will pay for the cost of renting while your home is being repaired from fire damage.

If someone hurts himself while on your property, he may demand you pay for damages. It's not as far fetched as it may sound. Let's say you've hired someone to clean out the gutters, and he falls off a ladder, badly injuring his neck. This is another common kind of homeowners insurance claim.

Homeowners insurance covers not just your house, but many of the possessions in your house, too. Computers, televisions, jewelry, and watches are often covered, although your policy may limit the amount you can claim. If you want to be sure an item is covered, call your insurance agent to ask. If it is not covered, you can often buy a rider to insure it. A rider is an add-on to your insurance policy. It gives you additional coverage for an additional cost.

# Disability Insurance

What would happen if you were injured or fell ill and could no longer work temporarily, or even permanently? How would you pay your bills? Afford groceries? Disability insurance covers this scenario. Your ability to earn a living is an important asset. Disability insurance protects that asset. Many people are covered under their employer's disability policy. This is a valuable job benefit.

# Avoid Scams

Insurance is one tool to reduce financial risk in your life, but what else can you do? At the top of your list should be learning how to be a smart consumer. A smart consumer is someone who is careful with her money and makes wise decisions. She takes the time to research a company before she does business with it. Before buying a product, she learns about what options are on the market and which product will best suit her needs. She reads the fine print before signing a contract.

One way to save money is to look for a deal, but some deals really are too good to be true. Trust your instincts. If it seems too good to be legitimate, it probably is a scam. If you feel bullied or pressured to make a decision, take that as a sign you should not be doing business with that person.

**Be Smart About Your Future**

# Guard Your Personal Information

A legitimate company would never call or e-mail you and ask you to disclose personal information. Your social security number, bank account and credit card numbers, passwords, and answers to security questions—for example, your mother's middle name—are all forms of personal information. Never give out personal information unless you are confident you are dealing with a legitimate company.

Even then, guard your personal information carefully. Companies are required by law to disclose how they use your personal information. You need to provide your employer with your social security number when you start a job, but as a rule, don't carry your social security card around in your wallet. Keep it somewhere safe.

# Do Your Research

A talented salesperson can convince you that you need the product he is selling. That is why you need to do your research ahead of time. Make sure you have all your questions answered before you buy an insurance policy. If you are not sure what questions to ask, then talk to someone you trust. A friend or family member who has experience buying that kind of policy can have some good advice. Ask him what you should be aware of and what he wished he'd known. You can benefit from his mistakes and the lessons he learned along the way. Being a smart consumer will set you on the path to leading a life of financial success.

**Here** is a money-saving tip: Buy your homeowners insurance from the same company that insures your car. Many companies offer a discount of 20 or 25 percent off your policy if you have multiple policies with them. You could also get a discount for having a security system. When you are shopping around for a policy, be sure to ask what discounts each company offers.

GOOD ¢

**You** get a desperate e-mail from a friend. She is traveling in Europe and got into a bit of trouble. Her wallet was stolen and she wants you to wire her some money. She'll repay you as soon as she gets home. You know for a fact that she is a trustworthy person, so you should help her out, right?

NON ¢

**Be** alert: This could be a scam. Your friend's e-mail account could've been hacked. Whenever anyone asks you for money, investigate.

40

# Do the Math

- You want to buy a used car and are deliberating between two. Both of them meet your needs but you are trying to decide which car will cost less.

- You drive 25 miles a day, 7 days a week. Gas prices are averaging $3.79 per gallon.

- Car #1 costs $7,500.
  Car #2 costs $9,000.

  Car #1 gets 18 miles per gallon (mpg).
  Car #2 is more fuel efficient and gets 32 mpg.

  You call your insurance agent to find out how much an insurance policy will cost for each of the cars. She informs you that the more fuel-efficient car qualifies for a discount of $125 per year.

  Which car will cost less over the course of a year? Is the answer the same if you keep the car for two years? Show your work.

# Glossary

**asset**—Something valuable that belongs to you.

**claim**—A demand for payment under an insurance policy.

**commodity**—A product that can be bought or sold.

**consumer**—A person who purchases goods or services.

**contract**—A written agreement between two parties that is enforceable by law.

**co-payment**—The amount you are responsible for paying at the time of service (your insurance pays the rest).

**deductible**—Amount of money the insured must pay before the insurer will pay the claim.

**financial planner**—A person who helps clients budget, save, and set financial goals.

**insurance**—The practice where a company agrees to pay for a loss or damage in exchange for payment.

**insurer**—The company providing the insurance.

Be Smart About Your Future

**insured**—The person buying the insurance policy from the insurance company.

**legitimate**—Legal, valid, genuine.

**liable**—At fault.

**limit of liability**—The most an insurance company agrees to pay in the case of a loss.

**Medicaid**—A government health insurance program for people with low incomes.

**mortgage**—A loan to pay for a house or land.

**premium**—The amount you (the insured) pay for an insurance policy.

**quote**—Estimate of how much a product, such as an insurance policy, will cost.

**reputable**—Having a good reputation; trustworthy.

**rider**—An add-on to an insurance policy that provides additional coverage for an additional cost.

**risk**—The possibility of suffering loss or harm.

**risk tolerance**—How much risk you are comfortable with.

# Learn More

## Books

Bellenir, Karen, ed. *Cash and Credit Information for Teens: Tips for a Successful Financial Life*. Detroit: Omnigraphics, 2009.

Butler, Tamsen. *The Complete Guide to Personal Finance: For Teenagers*. Ocala, Fla.: Atlantic Publishing Group, 2010.

Gagne, Tammy. *Teen Guide to Protecting and Insuring Assets*. Hockessin, Delaware: Mitchell Lane, 2013.

Scheff, Anna. *Shopping Smarts: How to Choose Wisely, Find Bargains, Spot Swindles, and More*. Minneapolis, Minn.: Twenty-First Century Books, 2012.

Be Smart About Your Future

## Internet Addresses

**The Mint.org: Fun Financial Literacy Activities**

<http://themint.org/>

**Department of Motor Vehicles: Teen Guide to Car Insurance**

<http://www.dmv.org/insurance/teen-guide-to-car-insurance.php>

**FTC—You Are Here: Where Kids Learn to Be Smart Consumers**

<http://www.ftc.gov/bcp/edu/microsites/youare-here/>

# Do the Math Answer Key

### Chapter 1: Hard Times Come Again No More

Answers will vary:

- By law, a motorcycle needs to be insured. Before you can drive it, it needs to be registered and that requires proof of insurance.
- A canoe does not need to be insured. For most people, a canoe is a nonessential item.
- An engagement ring, a laptop, and a new TV all should be insured under a homeowner's or renter's policy, but you can also purchase separate policies or extended warranties.
- For some items on the list, a reader could correctly argue that an item needs to be insured or that it doesn't. For example, people do not typically insure bicycles. However, you might want insurance on a bicycle if it were an expensive one and your main source of transportation to and from school or work. The idea is to get readers thinking about protecting their assets. Things that are essential or sentimental that cannot be replaced need to be insured.

### Chapter 2: Insurance to the Rescue

With Policy A, the student has to pay a thousand dollars for every INCIDENT in addition to the $300 annual premium. That could get expensive. Even though the premium is $250 more per year, Policy B is a better deal because if the student has an accident, he or she will only have to pay another $250 that year after paying the $550 premium.

### Chapter 3: Auto Insurance

Answers will vary. Here are three major differences between the two policies:

1. Policy #1 includes comprehensive insurance, which protects the vehicle from damage other than collision.
2. Policy # 2 has a higher deductible for collision insurance ($1,000 instead of $500).
3. Policy #2 costs $80 less than Policy #1.

I would choose Policy #2. Since we know the car is paid off and not worth very much, it is not worth buying comprehensive insurance. Since the owner is a

**Be Smart About Your Future**

student, saving $80 on the premium is important.
OR I would choose Policy #1. Although it costs $80 more, the extra coverage is worth it. If the car is stolen or damaged (other than in a collision), policy #2 would leave you without a car. Both answers are right—it is a matter of comfort level with risk.

## Chapter 4: Lowering Your Auto Insurance Costs
Determine the honor roll discount:
$650 × 10% = $65
Subtract the discount from your cost:
$650 − $65 = $585
Add your cost to your parents to get the total annual cost.
$585 + $1,500 = $2,085
Determine 3% of $2,085 to determine how much the defensive driving course saves. $2,085 × .03 = $62.55

## Chapter 5: Healthy, Wealthy, and Wise
First, you will need to pay the $25 co-pay. Then you will need to pay $500 of the $850 bill to reach your $1,000 annual deductible. $350 of the doctor's bill remains. Your insurance company covers 80% of that. $350 × .8 = $280. You owe the remaining $70. So your total is $25 + $500 + $70 = $595. Your insurance company pays $280.

## Chapter 6: Insurance Needs Throughout Your Life
First, determine how much gas you will need for each of the cars. You drive 25 miles a day, 7 days a week. 25 × 7 = 175 miles a week;
175 × 52 weeks per year = 9,100 miles per year.
Car #1 gets 18 mpg. 9,100 divided by 18 = 506 gallons of gas × 3.79 (average cost of gas) = $1,918.
Car #2 gets 32 mpg. 9,100 divided by 32 = 284 gallons of gas × 3.79 = $1,076.
Car #1 costs $7,500 plus $1,918 yearly cost of gas = $9,418.
Car #2 costs $9,000 plus $1,076 gas = $10,076 minus $125 savings on insurance =$9,951.
We don't have the exact amount of the insurance premiums, so we won't know exactly how much the car will cost—that's okay, we're just considering the difference.
Car #1 is cheaper for the first year, but if you factor in the second year, car #2 is cheaper.
Car #1 $9,418 + $1,918 (second year of gas) = $11,336
Car #2 $9,951 + $1,076 (second year of gas) = $11,027 minus second year insurance savings of $125 = $10,904.

**Do the Math Answer Key**

# Index

**Be Smart About Your Future**